ISLINGTON

South Library
115-117 Essex Road
London N1 2SL
Tel: 020 7527 7860

Library & Cultural Services

This item should be returned on or before the last date stamped below.
Users who do not return items promptly may be liable to overdue charges.
When renewing items please quote the number on your membership card.

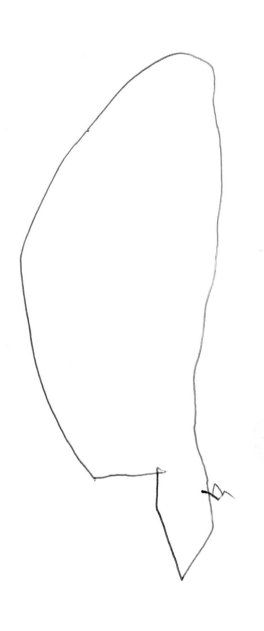

I LOVE YOU, FOOTBALL

Poems about the Beautiful Game

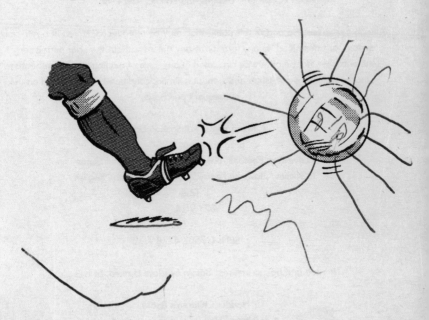

Published in Great Britain in 2003
by Hodder Wayland,
an imprint of Hodder Children's Books

Editor: Katie Orchard
Designer: Jane Hawkins

Cataloguing in Publication Data
Bradman, Tony, 1954–
I Love You, Football: Poems about the Beautiful Game
1. Soccer – Juvenile Poetry 2. Children's Poetry, English
I. Title
821.9'14

ISBN: 0 7502 4278 7

Printed and bound in Great Britain by Clays Limited, St Ives plc.

Hodder Children's Books
A division of Hodder Headline Limited
338 Euston Road, London NW1 3BH

I LOVE YOU, FOOTBALL

Poems about the Beautiful Game

Compiled by Tony Bradman

Illustrated by Steve Dell

For Martin –
only 91 grounds to go … T.B.

CONTENTS

THIS IS WHERE IT STARTS

This is the beginning of the great adventure,
This is the start of the dream;
This is where the future unfolds
for a premier football team.

The season's laid out like a street
where snow fell overnight
and you're waiting and eager to make your prints
and have a snowball fight,

Because nobody knows what's going to happen
The season's a sheet to scribble on
or a picture to paint, or some music to write
or a pitch to dribble on ...

The season's stretched out like a beach
where we can run and play
and we feel nothing's out of reach:
We'll be champions come May!

Because

This is the beginning of the greatest season
this is the start of the ride
fasten your seat belts, take the brakes off …
see you on the other side!

Ian McMillan

NEW KIT

And this is it.

Socks,

So long they reach

Above my knee.

Fold the tops over

Till they fit.

Shirt,

Breathe crisp nylon,

As it slips over my head.

Hitch up the sleeves

That stroke my knuckles.

Turn back the cuffs.

Shorts,

Not quite short enough,

'Growing room,' said Mum,

The usual stuff!

And now, at last,

The boots.

Inhale fresh leather,

Finger each stud,

Free of mud

For the last time in their lives.

Tie them tightly.

My mirror-twin grins,
Holds above his head
An invisible cup.
He gives me five,
My fingerprints slow to fade on the glass
And then
Dad's camera calls.
One foot on the ball,
Hands on hips, a cool pose;
Another, as if about to kick …
Delicious day. New kit.
Can't wait to get it
Caked in mud,
And yet …
When I take it off,
I sniff and fold,
For the last time.
Next week, it will slump
Awaiting a wash,
Crumpled on the floor,
Any old how,
Never quite the same
As it is right now.

Celia Warren

HERE FOR THE SEASON

It isn't the excitement as you shuffle through the gates
despite the choking mid-December fog.
It isn't swapping rotten jokes and meeting up with mates.
It isn't the cold drink or the hot dog.

It's not the Tannoy pumping ads and music through
  the ground
and giving out the team news for the day.
It's not the massive bag of sweets that someone passes round
between us as the game gets under way.

It's not my brother bringing his first girlfriend to the match
and turning a bright pink for no good reason.
It's not my grandad in his wheelchair who has come to watch
as he's done from a lad every season.

It's not the moment when the Number 9's about to score
and you hold your breath until the ball goes in
then suddenly the world is great – whatever's gone before,
your face is split by a gigantic grin.

It's not the tidal wave that ripples wildly through the crowd.
It's not the sense of being among friends.
It's not the hope of winning so that you can shout out loud.
It's all of these, however the match ends.

Jill.Townsend

GOLDEN

Last season I was awful
So I practised
I practised in sun, rain and un-seasonal snow
Through late spring, summer and early autumn
I practised shooting, passing and tackling
Watched the leaves turn brown and begin to fall
Now it's the first game of the season
In dull muddy September
But I have scored and everything is golden

Elinor Romans

TEAMSHEET

Sir has put the team up!

I cannot wait to play

I'm a natural kind of goalie

I've just been made that way.

I'm good in all positions,

As striker or midfield:

Quick, and hard

and pacey,

tricky and springheeled.

I'm a demon in the tackle,

A full back full of style

I overlap the winger,

Push passes full of guile.

My shooting's something special –

I swerve a ball with skill,

Keep the whole team ticking,

Give the crowd a thrill.

I'm a big star in the making

I'm a boy that's made for fame

And I'm off to read

The teamsheet ...

So look out for MY NAME.

Peter Dixon

THE NIGHT BEFORE THE MATCH

The night before the match
I lie awake in bed
With thoughts of what might happen
Whirling round my head.

What if there's an open goal
And somehow I fail to score?
What if I miss a penalty
And we lose instead of draw?

What If I miss a tackle
And give a goal away?
What if I get a red card?
What will people say?

What if I'm clean through
And I slip and tread on the ball?
What if I'm ill in the morning
And can't even play at all?

The night before the match
It's always the same.
Why can't I feel like Dad who says:
'Don't worry. It's only a game.'

John Foster

SPECTATORS

They bark instructions brief and blunt:
'Move!' 'Take it on!' 'Get in front!'
'Left, Kev!' 'Bad luck!' 'Run him, Chaz!"
'Go on!' 'Get your head up, Daz!'
'Get it! Get it! Get it!' 'Shoot!'
'In there, Brian!' 'Use your boot!'
'Wooooooo! Unlucky!' 'Come on, Town!'
'That's a corner!' 'Ref! He's down!'
'On your feet!' 'Don't hang about!'
'Get it out, lads! Get it out!'
'Offside, referee, you berk!'
'Hey there, linesman! Dirty work!'
'Off! Off! Off! Off!' 'Get the ball!'
'Give him some support there, Paul!'

'Yeahhh!' 'Go on!' 'Work 'em well!'

'Free Kick!' 'Take it!' 'Give 'em hell!'

'Make some chances!' 'Hey! Offside!'

'Run him, Robbie!' 'Ohhh, well tried!'

'Good header!' 'In there!' 'Play!'

'Get across him!' 'That's the way!'

'Got it!' 'Squeeze!' 'Now, put it in!'

'Get there, Gary!' 'Goooooal…!'

'We win!'

Nick Toczek

DAZZLING DEREK

That's my dad shouting at me
from the touchline
like he does every game we play.

I don't know why
I think we do quite well really
this week we're only losing 10-1
and I've scored three times
twice in my goal
and once in theirs –

not bad for a goalie.

Last week I was on the wing
It was brilliant
I nearly scored a million times
We still lost
But who was counting?

My dad was
he got really angry
there's no pleasing him.

What he really wants to do
is to shrink back to being small like me
slip on to the field
score the winning goal
with seconds to go
defeat staring us in the face
Dazzling Derek saves the day!

But he can't
so he jumps up and down on the touchline
shouts at me
mutters and kicks the grass
stubs his toe and yells
nearly gets sent off the field by the ref

where's the fun in that?

David Harmer

ONE BLADE OF GRASS

One blade of grass,
That's all there was
Between defensive suicide
And a brilliant pass –
Just one blade of grass.

One blade of grass,
That's all there was
Between rock steady hero
And stone dead zero –
Just one blade of grass.

One blade of grass,
That's all there was
Between poking the ball clear
And costing us dear –
Just one blade of grass.

One blade of grass,
That's what's made me
The kid whose hopes died,
The pariah of the side –
That
Championship-deciding,
Totally bad-tiding,
Heart-stopping,
Jaw-dropping,
Millimetre-thin,
Did me head in,
Lousy
Rotten
Blade of grass.

Alan Gibbons

MY OWN GOAL

Normally
Having something that's your own is good
Like your own Play Station
Your own passport
(where the photo's not you as a baby)
A room of your own
But an own goal?
That's in a different league

Owning your own goal is like
Getting nil for your homework
Every day of every week of every term
(when you've worked really hard, too)
Owning your own goal is like
Having your Uncle Stinkbreath to stay
Longer than just Sunday tea
(which is unbearable enough)

I suppose the only good thing about owning your own goal

Is that you don't have to own up to it

(everyone saw it, no mistake)

So the rest of the match you can focus on

The difference between your left and your right

The difference between your goal and theirs

And never putting the wrong two together

Ever

EVER again

Alison Boyle

THE FOOTBALLER

I take the pass

In the crowded

Playground

And kill it

The ball's tamed

To my foot

And goes where

I will it

To go

I take off

Slow, slide round

The tacklers

Past the skipping

Girls, dodge

The dinner ladies

Whirl on my heel

And maybe
I'll take a shot
From here
My view is clear
Through to
The coats we
Use as posts

Draw back
A foot and SHOOT!
Through the hole ...
GOAL!
The playground
Fades away ...
This is Wembley
On Cup Final Day

Tony Bradman

THE FOOTBALLER'S PRAYER

Our team

Which art eleven

Hallowed be thy game

Our match be won

Their score be none

On turf as we score at least seven

Give us today no daily red ... card

And forgive us our lost passes

As we forgive those who lose passes against us

Lead us not into retaliation

And deliver us from all fouls

For three is the kick-off

The power and scorer

For ever and ever

Full time

Paul Cookson

BEFORE THE MATCH

It's that special soccer moment:
When the teams come running out
And fifty-thousand voices blend
In one almighty shout;
And twenty-two, all clean and keen,
Fan out across the ground
And stretch their limbs and casually
Boot the ball around.
Now they're taking their positions,
Ninety minutes to go,
As the ref consults his stopwatch –
He's just about to blow.
It's all anticipation:
No one's lost and no one's won,
Triumphs, disappointments,
Thrills and spills are still to come.
No other time is quite as good –
It's the purest soccer heaven –
(Unless, of course, your favourite team
Knocks in six or seven!)

Eric Finney

BRISBANE ROAD

I used to go to watch Leyton Orient
(where the football's invariably neat and slick).
But what I loved most at Brisbane Road
Was the opposition goalie getting a goal-kick.

Aaaaaaaaaaaaah! went the crowd, as he ran up.
Then THUD off the ball would lurch
But, the moment that ball took off in the air,
the ground would go as silent as a church.

Not a whisper was made as the ball sailed up.
Not a sound as it twisted down like a coin.
But, the moment it touched the ground,
five thousand people yelled, 'BOING!'

Sean Taylor

LUCKY FLEECE

Round the side of KFC
Next shop after HMV
Past the van for ITV
is JJB
where Mum bought me my Lucky Fleece.
(It's a blue and red Puma, reversible with a zip
  front-pocket. Lush.)

I always meet up with Dale and Dale's Dad by Gate D.
Dale's dad always has a fag (bad for him) and a cup of tea,
I always have a coke and meat pasty,
And Dale always has a burger, no onions, and a 7-Up.
FA Cup sauce dribbling down his chin,
Dale says, 'We'll get hammered, we've got no chance.'

But, after we'd beaten Leeds 7-0
and so were still
in with a theoretical
shout at the Treble

31

Dale worked it out:
He said, 'We haven't lost since you got that fleece, and in fact,
   in recent weeks we've improved immensely.'

We talked about it on our way back out of Gate D.
And after the three minutes' walk to JJB
we went inside, up aisle three
wondering if he should get his mum to buy him one like me.
It could be double lucky,
but then again perhaps it might not be.

We stood standing for a long time
till Dale's dad finished off his fag (bad for him) and
   shouted in,
'C'mon lads: they'll be driving off the van from the ITV
And cashing up the tills at HMV
And all sold out of wings at KFC
By the time you've decided!'

But we had already decided
We'd decided that one Lucky Fleece was probably all they'd
ever stocked
in the JJB
next to HMV
after the KFC
Right close to the ground of the mighty City. (7-0 conquerors
    of Leeds United FC.)

And so we left it.

Stephen Foster

FINAL TERMLY REPORT

AT THE FOOTBALL REFEREEING ACADEMY

Eyesight – only four out of ten
Can't see the ball or the flag
Command of the rules – ten out of ten.
Common sense? There's the snag.
Personality – has mood swings
From timid and easily led
To gesticulating theatrically
And waving the yellow or red
Mathematics – inclined to confusion
Will muddle an eight and a three.
Congratulations. You passed with distinction
You're a new Premiership referee.

Roger Stevens

LOST

the penalty kick	was terrible
we trudged home	cursing to hell
losing the match	was bad enough
but the car	had been nicked as well

Lynne Taylor

HAIKU: SIX SOCCER SNAPSHOTS

A subtle through ball,
Perfect for both weight and line:
Defence left rooted.

Inevitable:
That free-kick, dipping, swerving,
Is bound for the net.

A cheeky back-heel,
Totally unexpected:
A dull game ignites.

Brain of the outfit:
The team revolves around him.
He's the play-maker.

A simple tap-in:
Over-eager, he fluffs it;
And clutches his head.

Penalty shoot-out:
The fate of nations hangs here.
A huge silence falls.

Eric Finney

I'M NOT A 'KEEPER

I used to play defender, but I didn't like it much
I tried to be a striker, but I barely got a touch
At training, there's no goalie, so we all take a turn
But I stopped the captain's thunderbolt and now there's
   no return.

The tournament was coming; still no 'keeper had arrived
I played in goal the first game and it seems that I survived
In fact, I quite enjoyed it, but I keep up my pretence
And say I'm not a 'keeper – so I'm moved into defence.

Well I lost count of the goals they scored, I played like I
   was blind
So when Coach says I'm back in goal, I actually don't mind
If we lose, we wave goodbye to any chances of the Cup
I think, 'I'm not a 'keeper,' but who would back me up?

I'm playing like a superstar! I'm player of the match!
I'm Van der Saar, I'm Dudek – I improve with every catch
We overcame the odds to win, despite a clueless ref
I say I'm not a 'keeper, but my team-mates have gone deaf.

We're up against the champions now; win, and we'll
    go through
I dream I score the winner but I know it won't come true
'Cause I sense what's coming just before the gloves land
    at my feet
I begin, 'I'm not …' then see the coach's face and
    know defeat.

Livvy Hanks

RAIN IN THE FINAL

Rain falls on the goalkeeper.
Rain falls on the crowd. Different rain!
Rain falls on the spot.

Rain falls on the striker as he places the ball.
Eight rain-soaked paces, back down the field.
Rain falls on every step.

Head up, runs forward, smashes the ball through the mud.
'Keeper dives for the ball, slips, too late, too wet, in the net.
And the sun shone down in the hearts of 273 home
   supporters.

My mate Gavin was the 'keeper.
And two more raindrops ran down his cheeks,
And dripped off his chin.

   Ian Larmont

PLAYING FOR THE SCHOOL

Looking lively, running out,
yellow strip, boots all shiny with dew.

November morning. Air brisk on cheeks,
on knees. Puffing clouds. Then sir

Shrilling his whistle and black rooks
coughing in the sticks of trees.

Booted ball, thudding, slithering
like a greased pig. Ninety minutes'

muscled battling. Mud all over.
Bruised warriors trudging in.

Tired. Winners. Hot as boiled eggs.

Matt Simpson

TEAM TALK

Marcus, don't argue with the ref.
Yes, he needs glasses
Yes, he should keep up with the play,
Yes, yes, he's a pawn
In some international betting syndicate
But don't argue with him.
He'll send you off.
And if he doesn't, I will.

Billy, you're the goalie – right?
Listen, you're allowed to use your hands
OK?
It's in the rules
It's legal.

Another thing
What's that you've got in the back of the net?
That carrier bag
I've seen it – what is it?
Hm.
Well, leave-it-a-lone
You can eat later.

Now then, Michael
You've got Charles outside you, OK?
Unmarked, OK?
I know he's only your brother
But pass to him.

Marcus, another thing
Don't argue with the linesman, either
Or me, for that matter
Or anybody
Just –
Just –
Just –
Marcus … shut up.

Kevin, a word.
Their number seven
You're supposed to be marking him
And he's scored five already, right?
Well that's … enough
Close him down.

So come on lads
The golden rules – remember?
Hold your positions
Run into space
Call for the ball
Play to the whistle
Pass only to members of your own team.

Last of all
NEVER GIVE UP
Thirteen-nil
Sounds bad, but it's not the end.
We can turn it round
We can get a result
It's a game of two halves.

So let's go out there –
And show 'em!

Billy … are you eating?

Allan Ahlberg

DEFENCE

The play's all at the front: the striker's fluffed it –
twice now I make it. He's off form today.
The pitch is in a bad state: there's a rough bit
I tamp down with my heel; that's the way.
Trot over to the goalie who looks bored.
That's why he's still clapping his gloves together –
to keep his concentration. – Hey, we've scored!
This is the most one-sided match ever.

Couldn't we see some action at this end?
Not that I want to pressurise the 'keeper
But it would help if the midfield could send
a few defensive passes a bit deeper.

At last, the opposition's broken through!
Let's close them down, show what we can do.

Jill Townsend

MIDFIELD

You need to be quite flexible and fit
in midfield cos whatever's going on
you're the front line. If you don't do your bit
the whole team falls apart and then we're done for.

For instance, when the opposition's 'keeper
takes a long goal kick and you see that one
of their men's just onside, you must run deeper,
shut him down so he can't go on a run.

Later, perhaps a loose ball comes your way.
You try to steal ten or twenty metres
then pass it when your striker's got away
and hope their 'keeper's coming out to meet us.
You hook it over him – the striker's waited
and just cracks in the goal that you created.

Jill Townsend

ATTACK

Even before the game's got under way
a few of our supporters chant my name
and, though it adds some pressure, I must say
it gets you really pumped up for the game.

Straight after kick-off someone slips the ball
towards me on the wing. I hook it round
my marker, sprint away – but when this tall
defender clatters in, I hit the ground.

Still, it's our free kick. Can we make it count?
(Unlucky not to get a penalty.)
The skipper bends it – just the right amount
to curl it past their defensive wall to me.
I swing round, place it – top left of the net!
An early goal, and one of my best yet!

Jill Townsend

THE SONG
OF THE SUB

I'm standing on the touchline
In my substitute's kit
As though it doesn't matter
And I don't mind a bit.

I'm trying to be patient
Trying not to hope
That my friends play badly
And the team can't cope.

I'm a sub, I'm a sub and I sing this song
And I'm only ever wanted when things go wrong.

When a boy has the measles
When a boy goes lame
The teacher turns to me
And I get a game.

When a boy gets kicked
Or shows up late
And they need another player
I'm the candidate.

I'm a sub, I'm a sub and I sing this song
And I'm only ever wanted when things go wrong.

I warm up on the touchline
I stretch and bend
And wonder what disasters
My luck will send.

If a boy got lost
Or ran away to France
If a boy got kidnapped
Would I get my chance?

I'm a sub, I'm a sub and I sing this song
And I'm only ever wanted when things go wrong.

I feel a bit embarrassed
That I'm not bothered more
When decisions go against us
And the other teams score.

I try to keep my spirits up
I juggle with the ball
And hope to catch the teacher's eye
It does no good at all.

Just a sub, just a sub till my dying day
And I only get a kick when the others can't play.

I'm standing on the touchline
On the very same spot
And it does really matter
And I do mind – a lot.

I think I'll hang my boots up
It's not the game for me
Then suddenly I hear those
   words:
You're on! I am? *Yippee!*

Allan Ahlberg

51

DENIS LAW

I live at 14 Stanhope Street,
Me Mum, me Dad and me,
And three of us have made a gang,
John Stokes and Trev and me.

Our favourite day is Saturday;
We go Old Trafford way
And wear red colours in our coats
To watch United play.

We always stand behind the goal
In the middle of the roar.
The others come to see the game –
I come for Denis Law.

His red sleeves flap around his wrists,
He's built all thin and raw,
But the toughest backs don't stand a chance
When the ball's near Denis Law.

He's a whiplash when he's in control,
He can swivel like an eel,
And twist and sprint in such a way
It makes defences reel.

And when he's hurtling for the goal
I know he's got to score.
Defences may stop normal men –
They can't stop Denis Law.

We all race home when full time blows
To kick a tennis ball,
And Trafford Park is our back-yard,
And the stand is next door's wall.

Old Stokesey shouts, 'I'm Jimmy Greaves,'
And scores against the door,
And Trev shouts: 'I'll be Charlton,' –
But I am Denis Law.

Gareth Owen

KICK IN THE TEETH

Dear Dino,
Welcome.
Just what City needs.
Now our dream, the Double,
Can come true.
I've stuck some pictures of you
On my wall,
Would love (hint, hint)
To have one more.
　　Yours,
　　　Anne (Your Greatest Fan)

Oh, Dino, thank you,
It's tremendous. Life-size!
I've stuck it next to
Where I lay my head.
Great game on Saturday –
How fast you ran.
City for the Cup!
All thanks to you.
    With love,
        Your devoted Anne

My Dearest Dino,
When you smiled at me
At the Leicester game
Just before you scored
For the second time,
I felt so proud.
Last thing at night
I kiss your photograph
Sleep tight, my darling.
    Anne,
        With *all* my love

Dino, you can't!
WE need you
HERE.
If I can't see you play
I know I'll die.
Oh, Dino, money
Isn't everything
Change your mind
OR I'LL RIP UP
YOUR PHOTOGRAPH.
    I mean it.
        ANNE

P. S. Before you leave
Please get me
Pellini's photo. *Signed.*

Frances Nagle

GEORGE BEST AND ME

George played to the sound of thunder
I played in a public park

George floated like a Spanish dancer
All I had was heart

Georgie lit the sky at Wembley
I never made the grade

Georgie filled the night with magic
I battled in the shade

But these are things that last forever
Memories that filled my heart
Separate worlds of football fever
So close yet very far apart.

David Clayton

BEFORE THE GAME

Socks: always left first, then right, *after* saying

United, backwards, three times: 'detinu, detinu, detinu'.

Pieces of orange to be handed out then

Eaten in the changing room, just before leaving. If

Raining, Robbo first, then in numerical order. If

Sunny, Snapper first, then in reverse numerical order.

Touch toes twice, in the centre circle, but

If we have to change ends, after the toss,

Touch toes, *outside* the centre circle, again.

If we win the toss, **never** change ends – **ever**.

Only tuck your shirt in just before kick-off:

Never leave your shirt hanging out – **ever**.

Superstitious – who says we're superstitious?

Mike Johnson

THE BALL TALKS IN ITS CHANGING ROOM

I'm the star really. I'm the one
the crowds have come to watch.
I don't let it worry me. Before the match
they check me carefully, make sure
I'm really fit. After all
I have to take more pressure
than the rest of them. And then
it's the usual jokes about
there being more hot air in
the commentators than in me,
and the ref puts his arm around
my shoulders and says he hopes
I'll have a good game, no need
for a substitute, and off we go
to lead the players out. No time
for second thoughts once we start:
I'm in the middle of it all the way
with everybody shouting for me,
cheering as I dodge around the tackles,

or slide out of reach of players
who just want to put the boot in.
The crowd is all for me, willing me on,
praying that I'll reach the net,
and when I do, roaring with delight.
I take it as my due. The lads are all right
but, when all's said and done, Desmond,
they'd be nothing without me.

Dave Calder

LEAVING EARLY

Come on, son
If we leave now
We can beat the traffic –
The ref's going to blow
Any minute
Anyhow

But we can't!
We might score!
I don't want to miss anything!
Besides,
Five quick goals for victory
It's not beyond the realms of
  possibility
– Is it?

Andrew Detheridge

SHAKESPEARE'S BOOTS

Shall I compare thee to a wintry afternoon?

Thou art more full of stinks and rank with mud:

Rough shots do rock the crossbar's sway

And the season's lease is all too short of fixture dates.

Sometime too loud the arbitrator's whistle shrills

And often is his brow with angry wrinkles lined;

And every pair from fair to middling doth decline

With kicks and in the cupboard, without dubbing, lies forgot.

But thy so lovely leather shall not crack nor fade

Nor lose possession of the ball so boldly won;

Nor shall the opposition brag you banged the leather orb too

　high, too wide.

Your laces caked with mud shall dry not rot in the eternal sun.

　　So long as fans shall cheer or sweaty feet can pound the sward,

　　No wife nor mother shall to thee display th'eternal red card.

Brian Moses

61

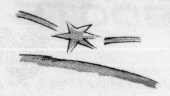

RHYTHM OF THE GAME

Football is the rhythm, and football is my life
Every day of every week of every year
From the stadia and stars to the experts in the bars
I will head, I will tackle, I will clear.

On the terraces at City I can feel the rhythm too
As I watch the reds run out on to the grass
While I sing up for my team, in a wild promotion dream
I'll accelerate, I'll dummy, I will pass.

Something keeps me going through the pain and
    through defeat
Cos I know I've got the magic in my soul
I can feel it in the freedom when the ball is at my feet
I will dribble, I will run, I'll head for goal.

And then back to the park again, where jumpers mark
    the posts
And kids become the players they adore
Now I know what I can be, with the rhythm deep in me
I will aim. I will shoot. I will score.

Livvy Hanks

SPEAK FOOTBALL

I am the reason for their boots.
Their boots are the reason I am.
It's this simple relationship
that sets a stadium howling
and rivets a foot to stardom.
Kicked around, my purpose fulfilled,
I provide work for a whistle
and take a breather in a net.
Then I rocket, I soar, I spin.
Even then I'll spare a thought
for some poor battered head.
I'm leather but I'm all heart.
Put me on the penalty spot
and learn from me this lesson.
There's a time to wave hands and scarves,
there's a time to be gutted –
a lump in the goal of the throat.

John Agard

GIRL FOOTBALLER

The ball soars and the ball flies.
The ball goes up. The ball goes in.
And the balls in your eyes,
are rolling and spinning,
spinning and rolling.
And the blood in your heart is singing.

You feel yourself whirl and twirl.
What a talented girl.
Nothing like this feeling you get
when the ball bulges in the back of the net.
No, you don't easily forget
the sweet sweet taste of a goal.
Replay it in your mind again:

Left foot in the air, flick,
straight to the back of the net.
Play it again and again
– the ball's beautiful roll to the goal.
Nothing like the soaring and roaring
when the plump ball hits the thin net.
And the sad blue goalie sits on the sad green grass.
The look on the slow face,
watching the ball go past, fast.
No chance. No chance. Watching the ball dance.
You dribble from the midfield down.
You get past three men.
You do a chip, a volley, you curl the ball.
You perm the air with your talent, and all
the fans sizzle and spark,
all the fans sing and dance,
football is one long romance
with the ball, with the ball and all.

You nutmeg the goalie like the goalie is a spice.
You get the ball in, not once, twice, but thrice!
Hat trick! You make the goalie feel sick.
So lie you down and roll in celebration.
You feel the team jump up on your back
Then you feel the whole nation,
Goggle-eyed in admiration.
You squeeze your fist,
Like this, like a kiss, to the wild crowd
And your football of a heart
   is bouncing and proud.

Jackie Kay

HIGH CURVING BALL

It's a high curving ball
   Coming in like a satellite,
      Spaceship,
        Meteorite,
         Jet.
          And I've found space
           Should be an ace goal.
          When my head connects
          They won't even sniff it,
          Defenders out of it.
        'S'mine this time
        And it's falling

and
I'm diving
and
BANG!
It's there, in the net!
Goalie staring, upset
Shouting:
'It's not my fault!'
But I'm up, up and away
Floating …
Cloud, balloon, in my cocoon
Of glory.

Ivan Jones

THE GOALIE MAKES HIS EXCUSES

The rain came down like two-inch nails,
then the hail came in bucketfuls.

I was pelted till my skin began to sting.
The pitch was all crunchy.

Couldn't see five yards. The ball just appeared
from nowhere. Went in the back of the net all right

but didn't see who scored! Hard to keep
eyes open in that brute wind!

Bones growled, muscles groaned.
I was glad afterwards ... it was like

Being massaged all over ... to get,
thank goodness, under the steaming hot shower!

Matt Simpson

FOOTBALL AT SLACK

Between plunging valleys, on a bareback of hill
Men in bunting colours
Bounced, and their blown ball bounced.

The blown ball jumped, and the merry-coloured men
Spouted like water to head it.
The ball blew away downwind –

The rubbery men bounced after it.
The ball jumped up and out and hung on the wind
Over a gulf of treetops.
Then they all shouted together, and the ball blew back.

Winds from fiery holes in heaven
Piled the hills darkening around them
To awe them. The glare light
Mixed its mad oils and threw glooms.
Then the rain lowered a steel press.

Hair plastered, they all just trod water
To puddle glitter. And their shouts bobbed up
Coming fine and thin, washed and happy

While the humped world sank foundering
And the valleys blued unthinkable
Under depth of Atlantic depression –

But the wingers leapt, they bicycled in air
And the goalie flew horizontal

And once again a golden holocaust
Lifted the cloud's edge, to watch them.

Ted Hughes

CUP FINAL DAY, 1961

Pete supported Burnley,
but Spurs were all that I cared about.
We knew, by the end of Cup Final day
that one of us would be leaping about
and one of us would be quiet,
unless, of course, it went to a replay.

So that Saturday in May
we sat down to watch
the match of the year.

And Spurs got off to a dream start
when Jimmy Greaves scored an early goal
and I was ecstatic
till Pete knocked me back, 'Sit down,'
he said, 'Shut up, watch the match.'

It was nothing much till the second half,
then Burnley scored and Pete went mad,
but just as he sat back down again

it was Bobby Smith with a cracker of
   a goal
for Spurs, 'Don't shout so much,'
my mother called, 'the teams can't
   hear you.'

Then just ten minutes before the end
Blanchflower booted a penalty
and Spurs stayed in front 3-1.

I leapt around, jumped up and down,
ran round the room holding the cup,
listened to the sound of the Wembley
crowd as I took my victory lap.

'You're daft, you are, you're crazy,'
Pete said, but I jeered him all the
way to the door.
'3-1,' I crowed, 'I told you so.'

Then, 'What shall we do tomorrow?' I called
but he didn't turn around, just walked away,
and next day too it was like a wall
had suddenly grown between us.

He kept it up for a week or so,
wouldn't speak, kept clear of me,
and it took me a week to understand
that a game of ball didn't matter at all,
it's friendship that really counts.

So I went across and knocked on Pete's door,
'I'm sorry that your team lost,' I said.
He shrugged. 'Doesn't matter any more,
there's always next year, we'll beat you
for sure.'

'I expect so,' I said,
fingers crossed
behind my back.

Brian Moses

NOT LIKE BEING THERE

You'd rather watch it on telly, you say,
From your favourite comfy chair?
Yes, I know you'll get re-runs and expert opinion –
But it's not like *being there*.

You say you get cold when you go to a match?
So wear your scarf and your bobble hat!
And the half-time refreshments are awful?
It's no good being put off by that.

Yes, I know that the parking is tricky
And the forecast predicts a downpour –
But a pitch like a mud heap suits City:
They might just get a goalless draw.

If they're going to avoid relegation
You won't help them sitting here.
City need folks through the turnstiles;
Besides: *think of the atmosphere!*

Eric Finney

THE WEMBLEY WAY

(IN MEMORY OF THE OLD WEMBLEY STADIUM: THE HOME OF FOOTBALL FOR MANY YEARS)

One sunny Saturday in May
we joined the crowds on Wembley Way.

We joined the fans all walking up
to watch the Final of The Cup.

We saw the banners held up high
and saw the flags against the sky.

The fans all joked and larked about,
and 'Wembley! Wembley!' was the shout.

'Come on, you Blues!' 'Come on, you Reds!'
We saw huge coloured hats on heads.

Both sets of fans let laughter ring
and you should just have heard them sing.

There was no nastiness, just fun
as all the fans smiled in the sun.

The game was great. Ten out of ten.
But nothing matched the friendship when

up for The Cup on Final day
we joined the crowds on Wembley Way.

Wes Magee

ATTENDING
A FOOTBALL
MATCH

It sneaked past watchful attendants,
warned to be on the look-out for It
among the male together-noise.
White faces on dark clothes
cohered, shading the terracing
to the anonymous crouch of a crowd.

The ninepin players trotted in.
Kinetic muscles in play,
and Matt, John, Jock and Wullie
bounced on their excitement's cheers.

But as the ball began to score
goals spent in a stretched net,
It wedged Itself between the roars
of the single-backed, two-minded thing,
for *game*, insinuated *name*,
a syllableless, faceless feeling
of nothing words identified.

Then suddenly It broke loose –
bottles hit fists and screams.
Police tore the crowd apart
to get It. It eluded them.

From spectators crushed by shock,
a swearing vanful of louts,
the cut-up quiet in hospitals,
no real evidence could be taken.
Charges were, of course, preferred –
disorderly conduct, obstructing the police –
but no one found out what It was,
or whose It is, or where It came from.

Maurice Lindsay

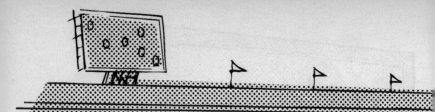

MONDAY 26TH NOVEMBER 7.50 P.M.

Our kid, Jamie, limps into view
Thin as a blade (but not as sharp).
Fanfared by floodlight and tannoys.

The swelling crowd outstretch their scarves
They swallow him up.
Look, there he is!
Spat out in the centre circle
Our kid, Jamie, gulping like a fish.

A smile breaks through
Wide as a goal.
His glass rims glint, reflecting glory
As he claps them clapping.
All Big Screen Magnification.

See the Captain wink at our kid,
  Jamie,
Lurching forward to take a shot.
And again.
Go on!
And another
Yes!

Now back to centre spot.
Handshakes
Pennants swapped.
Job done and off he goes.
Our kid, Jamie, Premier Mascot
Looks behind, one last time
And waves to the world.

Rachel Rooney

THE WORLD'S BEST

My dad's the world's best.
He's a football referee.
He referees internationals
From a seat on our settee.

An hour before the kick-off
He gets changed into his kit.
He then inspects the room
And tells us where to sit.

As we watch the pre-match build-up,
He waits beside the door,
Until the teams come out,
Then he strides across the floor.

He stands to attention
While the national anthems play,
Then takes his seat on the settee
As the game gets underway.

His eagle eyes spot every foul
The opposition makes.
He's very quick to point out
The real ref's mistakes.

He won't stand for any nonsense.
On a dissent he's very hard.
If we challenge his decisions,
He shows us a red card.

But sometimes he forgets
His self-appointed role
By letting out a mighty roar
When England scores a goal.

John Foster

FRIDAY MORNING

LAST TWO LESSONS
IS GAMES DAY

We straggle in two's
Down Endbutt Lane to the playing fields,
In a gap-toothed murmuring line
Filling the pavement.
Mr Pearson strides out in front
The ball tucked firmly under one arm,
His head bent.

We avoid lampposts
And young mothers pushing prams,
Sometimes walk gammy-legged in gutters
Or scuffle through damp leaves.
The morning is filled
With laughter-tongued and pottering mongrels;
Old men tending bare borders
Slowly unbend
And lean upon their brooms to watch us pass.
Their wives in flowered pinnies
Peer through the lace curtains
Of unused front rooms.

At the pitch
We change in the old pavilion
That smells of dust and feet
And has knot-holes in the boarding.
Someone
From another class
Has left
One
Blue and white sock behind
The lads shout about other games
And goals and saves and shots
Or row about who'll wear red or blue.
Pearson blows exasperation
Briskly through his whistle,
'Come on lads, let's be having you.'

With eighteen a side
We tear after the ball shouting,
Longing to give it a good clean belt,
Perform some piece of perfection –
Beat three sprawling backs in a mazy dribble,

Race full pelt on to a plate-laid-on pass
And crack it full of hate and zest
Past the diving goalie to bulge the net.
But there is no net
And we have to leg it after the ball
To the allotments by the lane
To start the game again.

Afterwards,
Still wearing football socks,
Studded boots slung on my shoulder,
I say 'Tarrah' to Trev
At Station Road and drift home
Playing the game again.
Smoke climbs steep from neat red chimneys;
Babies drool and doze
And laugh at the empty sky.
There is the savour of cabbage and gravy
About the Estate and the flowers do not hear
The great crowd roaring me on.

      Gareth Owen

HALL OF SHAME

There was a dirty footballer
Played for a dirty team
In a dirty, dirty, dirty, dirty match
The dirtiest ever seen.

Now that footballer
Lies in a hospital bed
Because an even dirtier footballer
Kicked him in the head.

That even dirtier footballer
Thought this was just a laugh
Till the referee sent him off
To an early bath.

So, don't go playing dirty
Don't spoil the beautiful game
Let dirty, dirty, dirty, dirty,
Footballers remain
In the dirty, dirty, dirty, dirty,
Football hall of shame.

Jeremy Davies

THE NUTMEG RAP

Sir keeps getting at me
all the while
yelling 'Get stuck in!'
but that's not my style
'Put yourself about
get your tackles in!'
but I play for kicks
I don't play to win

Me, I like a move
that ebbs and flows
no sense in burning out
and getting comatose
Me, I go for tricks you
don't learn in classes
cheeky chips, banana kicks
and sumptuous passes

I like to juggle the ball
from side to side
dazzle defenders
leave 'em mesmerised
like to lean and weave
and hypnotise
leave 'em open-mouthed
– catching flies!

I really couldn't care
we're losing 6 to 3
if we're playing the game
the way it's meant to be
winning's for losers
and bruisers and wallies
Me, I'm the prince of fabulous volleys

I'm not hard as nails
I'm cool as ice
I don't go chasing pain
don't do sacrifice
I like my limbs
the way they are
I don't need to flash
no six-inch scar

All the world's my valley,
the pitch, the park
the back-street alley
I don't play to kill
I play to thrill
I don't do war
I do soccer ballet

I'm a dancer
not a soldier
I'm like Gianfranco Zola
I don't do defence
it's too intense
if I bust my knees
where's the recompense?

So keep your growls and
fouls and your chainsaw tackles
keep your digs and dives
and rising hackles
give me a wicked lob
a subtle mix
I'm the Nutmeg King
the jack of all tricks
and flicks

I'm an actor
not a tractor
that's the crucial factor
don't make me play rough
I don't do that huff and puff stuff
I stay cool
as a rule

I'm sleeker than
a cheetah
I'm a wicked offside beater
I love the wind
in my face
a pass hit at pace
a goal scored with grace
by an ace

Jonathan Kebbe

THE APPRENTICE

I had a dream of glory –
apprenticeship for me!
But it's a different story,

the reality.
Most mornings I clean boots
till I can guarantee

even the substitutes'
will look as good as new –
a fact the coach disputes

and forces me to do
some more before youth training
which starts at half past two.

And why's it always raining –
the best bit of the day – ?
But still, I'm not complaining:

I just wish we could stay
out longer, practice scoring,
learning how to play.

They seem to be ignoring
our skills and it's a sin;
and tactics talks are boring.

I could help them win!
But still they always say
learn some discipline

before we let you play.

Jill Townsend

FALLING STAR

When Danny had just learnt to crawl
His dad bought him his first football
He loved it.

Then he walked and got the trick
Of giving that big ball a kick
Terrific!

By the time he was four
He could dribble, pass and score
Fantastic!

When everybody saw him play
They said You'll be a star one day
Believe it.

For junior school and Sunday team
Danny played like a dream
Brilliant.

Top team scouts came to each game
Each of them thought just the same
Let's sign him.

He joined a club and very soon
They'd promised him the sun and moon
A future.

School slipped slowly out of sight
He thought of football day and night
Obsessive.

Youth team games were hard and tough
And Danny wasn't good enough
Disaster.

It broke his heart but it was true
His professional days were through
They dumped him.

Danny learned to smoke and swear
To show them that he didn't care
Who needs them?

Football's cruel, unforgiving
Not that many make a living
Ask Danny.

David Harmer

I'M FOR ...

I'm for the team that's fast and clean

not dirty or mean, I'm for the team

that doesn't stop running

whose passes are stunning

and the ball seems to know

just where it should go

to fall smooth and neat at the next twitching feet

as they sweep down the pitch

switching wings as they race

to make space or run rings

round an outpaced defence. I'm for

the team whose strength is skill,

that will twist and swerve

with control and nerve

as they dribble through the middle

but don't fiddle, fight or quibble

with the ref

wasting time and breath. I'm

for the team who play so well

that my mind and heart

are lost in their art

so I don't scream or yell

but gasp in delight and grin.

(I don't care if they win.)

Dave Calder

TELLING IT TO THE GODS

I lose my rag sometimes, see,
when I'm in a game.
I know I shouldn't,
and my dad, watching, gives me hell.

But I'm tight inside,
wound up, coiled up, a spring,
a firework, fused, waiting to blow.
The whistle goes and I'm a rocket.

I hear the crowd screaming,
and even if it's only my mates,
or everyone's dads yelling,
rooting for us, I go ballistic.

The other side are the enemy.
So when they hold me,
pulling my strip when the ref can't see,
I'm battling for my life.

I know I'm good, got promise,
but losing my cool is spoiling my chances.
Oh, God, let me make the team.
I want it so bad.

Narissa Knights

FOOTY POEM

I'm an ordinary feller six days of the week
But Saturday turn into a football freak.
I'm a schizofanatic, sad but it's true
One half of me's red, and the other half's blue.

I can't make me mind up which team to support
Whether to lean to starboard or port
I'd be bisexual if I had time for sex
Cos it's Goodison one week and Anfield the next.

But the worst time of all is Derby day
One half of me's at home and the other's away
So I get down there early in me usual place,
With me rainbow scarf and me two-tone face.

And I'm shouting for Liverpool, the Reds can't lose
'Come on de Everton' – 'Gerrin dere Blues'
'Give it to _____*' – 'Worra puddin'
'King of der Kop' – All of a sudden – Wop!
'Goal!' – 'Offside!'

    *Insert name of Anfield hero.

And after the match as I walk back alone
It's argue, argue all the way home
Some nights when I'm angry I've even let fly
An given meself a poke in the eye.

But in front of the fire watchin' 'Match of the Day'
Tired but happy, I look at it this way:
Part of me's lost and part of me's won
I've had twice the heartaches – but I've had twice the fun.

Roger McGough

THE GREATEST TEAM NEVER TO WIN A TITLE

Their challenge fell away at Easter
With games against Leeds, Man U and Arsenal.
How cruel the fixture computer can be.

They lost the FA Cup Final Replay
On penalties, having led till injury time.
Their Captain wakes in nightmares
With his hands about to grasp the trophy.

The greatest team never to win a title:
Their ghosts cry in the bars and clubs of England
Remembering the early leads they squandered
The defence that was almost invincible
The striker sold at the wrong time of the season
The goalkeeper who was not quite brilliant enough.

Tony Lewis-Jones

THE CHOOSING

It's in the lap of the gods
Exactly who you are drawn to
The magical moment that decided
Whether you're red, white or blue
You don't choose the football team
The football team chooses you

The highs and the lows, the thick and the thin
Allegiance will always shine through
United you stand together for ever
The heart forever is true
You don't have to choose the football team
The football team chooses you

You are special, you are selected
One of the chosen few
A bond that cannot be broken
There's nothing at all you can do
You don't choose the football team
The football team chooses ... you

Paul Cookson

FOOTBALL CRAZY

We're football crazy
We're football mad
We are the fans who follow our team
Through good times and through bad.

We are the fans, some young, some old
Who come each week and brave the cold.

We are the fans who fill the ground
With songs and chants, oh, what a sound.

We are the fans from East and West
Who really think our team's the best.

We are the fans who love football
United we stand and united we fall.

We're football crazy
We're football mad
We are the fans who follow our team
Through good times and through bad.

Richard Caley

supporters_log.on

www.unitedplc

welcome to the website

our information's free

log on to discover

how successful clubs are run

shop on-line and meet the stars

see the cups they've won

browse through all the merchandise

our loyal fans requested

read the manager's account

of the night he was arrested

we encourage our great followers

to surf the net in red

buy our clothes and spread the word
support with heart and head
anything is possible
just grab your mouse and flick it
we offer you free access –
just don't request a ticket
for
a
match
as they are **sold out**
to businessmen and their wives
who don't know the captain's name

anyone want to log off?

Daphne Kitching

SATURDAY EVENING

From Dundee to Dover
The games are all over
And those who have lost
Will be counting the cost ...

I know it'll vex 'em
In Rochdale and Wrexham.
At Clydebank and Clyde
They'll have cried and have cried.
They'll be glumly pathetic
At Charlton Athletic,
But moodily manly
At Accrington Stanley.

Cos nobody likes to lose.
They stand and stare at their shoes.
They're gobsmacked and gutted
Like they've been head-butted.
Life's not worth a carrot,
They're as sick as a parrot
And struggle to cope with the news.

At Manchester City
They're full of self-pity.
At Port Vale they're pale,
At Alloa, sallower,
Sullen in Fulham,
Morose at Montrose,
And Bradford and Burnley
Just sulk taciturnly.

Cos nobody likes to lose.
They stand there and stare at their shoes.
They're gobsmacked and gutted
Like they've been head-butted.
Life's not worth a carrot.
They're sick as a parrot
And struggle to cope with the news.

Nick Toczek

FOOTBALL

In Croatia
I played for a team in
Division One
I was quite good
and I was happy

Then,
I had to leave my country
and my team
so
I came to England

It was different
No home, no language, no football
Then
Someone asked me
'Do you like football?'

I smiled
'Of course'
and soon
I was playing in a team
for 'Hempstead Fieldings'

I
could not speak
I
could not understand
but, who cares?
I could play football

Dragan Medic

A MANAGER'S TALE

AT THE START OF THE SEASON
WE WERE THIRD FROM THE TOP
NOW WE NEED THESE POINTS
TO AVOID THE DROP.

WE'D WIN THIS MATCH
I'D SWORN ON OATH
IT WAS A GAME OF TWO HALVES
BUT WE LOST THEM BOTH.

AS MANAGER HERE
I MUST TAKE THE BLAME
AS I'VE SAID BEFORE
IT'S A FUNNY OLD GAME.

I'M AS SICK AS A PARROT
WHAT MORE CAN I SAY?
THE LADS DONE GOOD
BUT IT WASN'T OUR DAY.

WE'LL BE BACK NEXT SEASON
JUST WAIT AND SEE
THE PLAYERS, THE FANS
AND, HOPEFULLY, ME.

Richard Caley

AFTER THE GAME

My shirt all clammy with sweat
Shorts all caked with mud,
Are not coming off just yet!
I might even wear them for good!

My skin is tingly and hot,
Breathing's furious and fast,
Muscles are tight as a knot:
It's a feeling I just want to last.

The minute I ran on to play
I felt I was riding high:
I want to relive this day
Until the moment I die,

To remember us attacking,
Hurtling down the right,
The sound of leather smacking,
Their goal coming into sight,

Then two minutes before the whistle blew,
The ball came bouncing up,
The belt I gave it! I absolutely *knew*
We had finally won the CUP!

Matt Simpson

FOOTBALLERS IN THE PARK

December. Wet Saturday in the park.
It's late afternoon and it's growing dark

as a bevy of boys play their football game.
Most wearing baggy shorts. One goalie's lame.

Posts are old jerseys and hand-me-down coats;
the boys' boots are bulky as rowing boats.

Leather ball's sodden and heavy with mud.
It thumps a boy's face with a squelchy thud

and blood dribbles down from a nose struck numb:
a fat lad stunningly skids on his bum.

One boy shivers in his 'Wednesday' shirt,
the collar's ripped and he's plastered with dirt.

The game rattles on; chill drizzle sets in.
The wind in the trees makes a Cup Final din.

Distantly, lights shine on the wet street
unnoticed by boys whose thundering feet

are playing the game. But the hour grows late.
Here comes the park keeper to padlock the gate.

And the year is 1948.

Wes Magee

THE FOOTBALL GHOSTS

At night, when the stadium is empty,
When the grass in the moonlight is silver-grey,
When the goals look like hungry fishing nets,
   It is then the old ghosts play.

When all the crisp packets and fag-ends
And the drink cans have been swept up,
And the crowd has left, and the gates are locked,
   They play for the Phantom Cup.

Thin clouds drift across the face of the moon,
The grass stirs, a preeping whistle sounds,
And silent invisible spectators
   Throng the deserted stands.

And twenty-two ghosts in long-legged shorts
Dance the ball across the silvered grass,
A ball you can almost see, the old game –
    Run, dribble and pass.

Pale shades and shadows, heroes of bygone days,
Under the gaze of the moon, sidestep and swerve,
And crowds silently cheer as the ball floats
    Goalwards in an unseen curve.

Gerard Benson

THE BEAUTIFUL GAME

I will play you on the soft sand
Where great Rio meets the sea
I will play you in my bare feet
Leave my shantytown behind

I will play you in the back streets
With a garage for my goal
I will play you in my work clothes
Get some fresh air to my lungs

I will play you in the schoolyard
Run my heart out till the bell
Scuff my shoes and rip my trousers
When I get home I'll get hell

I will play you at Old Trafford
With a red shirt on my back
Feel the pride of being 'United'
Feel the pride of being the best

I am black and white and yellow
I am boy and I am girl
I am famous
I am no one

I love you, football

I am the World

David Clayton

ACKNOWLEDGEMENTS

John Agard for *Speak Football*;

Allan Ahlberg for *Team Talk* and *The Song of the Sub* from *Friendly Matches* by Allan Ahlberg (Viking, 2001) © Allan Ahlberg, 2001;

Gerard Benson for *The Football Ghosts*;

Alison Boyle for *My Own Goal*;

Tony Bradman for *The Footballer*. Reproduced by permission of The Agency (London) Ltd. Copyright © Tony Bradman 1989. First published in *All Together Now* by Viking. All rights reserved and enquiries to The Agency (London) Ltd 24 Pottery Lane, London W11 4LZ;

Dave Calder for *The Ball talks in its Changing Room* © Dave Calder, 1993, *I'm For ...* © Dave Calder 2000. Reprinted by permission of the author;

Richard Caley for *Football Crazy* and *A Manager's Tale*;

Paul Cookson for *The Footballer's Prayer* and *The Choosing*;

David Clayton for *George Best and Me* and *The Beautiful Game*;

Andrew Detheridge for *Leaving Early*;

Jeremy Davies for *Hall of Shame*;

Peter Dixon for *Teamsheet*;

Eric Finney for *Before the Match*, *Not Like Being There* and *Haiku: Six Soccer Snapshots*;

Stephen Foster for *Lucky Fleece*;

John Foster for *The Night Before the Match* © 2001 John Foster from *Word Wizard* (Oxford University Press) and *The World's Best* © 2003 John Foster, included by permission of the author;

Alan Gibbons for *One Blade of Grass*;

Livvy Hanks for *I'm Not a Keeper* and *Rhythm of the Game*;

David Harmer for *Dazzling Derek* and *Falling Star*;

Ted Hughes for *Football at Slack* from *Remains of Elmet* (Faber and Faber Ltd);

Mike Johnson for *Before the Game*;

Ivan Jones for *High Curving Ball* © Ivan Jones, 2003. Reprinted by permission of the author;

Jackie Kay for *Girl Footballer* from *The Frog Who Dreamed She Was an Opera Singer* (Bloomsbury);

Jonathan Kebbe for *The Nutmeg Rap*;

Daphne Kitching for *supporters_log.on*;

Narissa Knights for *Telling It to the gods*;

Ian Larmont for *Rain in the Final*;

Tony Lewis-Jones for *The Greatest Team Never To Win A Title*;

Maurice Lindsay for *Attending a Football Match*;

Wes Magee for *The Wembley Way* and *Footballers in the Park* © Wes Magee;

Roger McGough for *Footy Poem*. Reprinted by permission of PFD on behalf of: Roger McGough;

Ian McMillan for *This is Where It Starts*, www.ian-mcmillan.co.uk;

Dragan Medic for *Football*;

Brian Moses for *Cup Final Day 1961* and *Shakespeare's Boots*;

Frances Nagle for *Kick in the Teeth*;

Gareth Owen for *Denis Law* and *Friday Morning Last Two lessons is Games Day*, © Gareth Owen 2000. Reproduced by permission of the author c/o Rogers, Coleridge & White Ltd., 20 Powis Mews, London W11 1JN;

Elinor Romans for *Golden*;

Rachel Rooney for *Monday 26th November 7.50pm*;

St Peter's High School for *Football*;

Matt Simpson for *Playing for the School*, *The Goalie Makes his Excuses* and *After the Game*;

Roger Stevens for *Final Termly Report At the Football* and *Refereeing Academy*;

Lynne Taylor for *A Game of Two Halves*;

Sean Taylor for *Brisbane Road* © Sean Taylor;

Nick Toczek for *Spectators* and *Saturday Evening*;

Jill Townsend for *Here for the Season*, *Defence*, *Midfield*, *Attack* and *The Apprentice*;

Celia Warren for *New Kit* © Celia Warren 2003.

ABOUT TONY BRADMAN

Tony Bradman is the author of many popular children's books, and has recently published two novels about a football team: *Under Pressure* and *Bad Boys*. Tony has also edited many successful short story and poetry anthologies.

Other Hodder Wayland poetry collections
compiled by Tony Bradman include:
All Aboard the Toy Train
Here Come the Heebie Jeebies
The Hairy Hamster Hunt
Off to School
Wild and Wonderful!

FULL TIME